My dog's Medical Record

SOUTHWELL SAIRA

DOG INFORMATIONS

NAME

_____

BIRTH DATE: _____ / _____ / _____

BREED: _____

COLOR(S): _____

EYE COLOR: _____

ALLERGIES&ILLNESS: _____

BLOOD TYPE: _____

OTHER DETAILS: _____

VET INFO:

NAME: _____

ADDRESS: _____

PHONE: _____

E-MAIL: _____

VACCINATION RECORD:

DATE	AGE	VACCINE	NEXT VACCINE DATE
___/___/_____	_____	_____	___/___/_____
___/___/_____	_____	_____	___/___/_____
___/___/_____	_____	_____	___/___/_____
___/___/_____	_____	_____	___/___/_____
___/___/_____	_____	_____	___/___/_____
___/___/_____	_____	_____	___/___/_____
___/___/_____	_____	_____	___/___/_____
___/___/_____	_____	_____	___/___/_____
___/___/_____	_____	_____	___/___/_____
___/___/_____	_____	_____	___/___/_____
___/___/_____	_____	_____	___/___/_____

VACCINATION RECORD:

DATE	AGE	VACCINE	NEXT VACCINE DATE
___/___/_____	_____	_____	___/___/_____
___/___/_____	_____	_____	___/___/_____
___/___/_____	_____	_____	___/___/_____
___/___/_____	_____	_____	___/___/_____
___/___/_____	_____	_____	___/___/_____
___/___/_____	_____	_____	___/___/_____
___/___/_____	_____	_____	___/___/_____
___/___/_____	_____	_____	___/___/_____
___/___/_____	_____	_____	___/___/_____
___/___/_____	_____	_____	___/___/_____
___/___/_____	_____	_____	___/___/_____
___/___/_____	_____	_____	___/___/_____
___/___/_____	_____	_____	___/___/_____
___/___/_____	_____	_____	___/___/_____
___/___/_____	_____	_____	___/___/_____
___/___/_____	_____	_____	___/___/_____
___/___/_____	_____	_____	___/___/_____
___/___/_____	_____	_____	___/___/_____
___/___/_____	_____	_____	___/___/_____

VACCINATION RECORD:

DATE	AGE	VACCINE	NEXT VACCINE DATE
___/___/_____	_____	_____	___/___/_____
___/___/_____	_____	_____	___/___/_____
___/___/_____	_____	_____	___/___/_____
___/___/_____	_____	_____	___/___/_____
___/___/_____	_____	_____	___/___/_____
___/___/_____	_____	_____	___/___/_____
___/___/_____	_____	_____	___/___/_____
___/___/_____	_____	_____	___/___/_____
___/___/_____	_____	_____	___/___/_____
___/___/_____	_____	_____	___/___/_____
___/___/_____	_____	_____	___/___/_____
___/___/_____	_____	_____	___/___/_____
___/___/_____	_____	_____	___/___/_____
___/___/_____	_____	_____	___/___/_____
___/___/_____	_____	_____	___/___/_____
___/___/_____	_____	_____	___/___/_____
___/___/_____	_____	_____	___/___/_____
___/___/_____	_____	_____	___/___/_____
___/___/_____	_____	_____	___/___/_____
___/___/_____	_____	_____	___/___/_____
___/___/_____	_____	_____	___/___/_____

VACCINATION RECORD:

DATE	AGE	VACCINE	NEXT VACCINE DATE
___/___/_____	_____	_____	_____	___/___/_____
___/___/_____	_____	_____	_____	___/___/_____
___/___/_____	_____	_____	_____	___/___/_____
___/___/_____	_____	_____	_____	___/___/_____
___/___/_____	_____	_____	_____	___/___/_____
___/___/_____	_____	_____	_____	___/___/_____
___/___/_____	_____	_____	_____	___/___/_____
___/___/_____	_____	_____	_____	___/___/_____
___/___/_____	_____	_____	_____	___/___/_____
___/___/_____	_____	_____	_____	___/___/_____
___/___/_____	_____	_____	_____	___/___/_____
___/___/_____	_____	_____	_____	___/___/_____
___/___/_____	_____	_____	_____	___/___/_____
___/___/_____	_____	_____	_____	___/___/_____
___/___/_____	_____	_____	_____	___/___/_____
___/___/_____	_____	_____	_____	___/___/_____
___/___/_____	_____	_____	_____	___/___/_____
___/___/_____	_____	_____	_____	___/___/_____
___/___/_____	_____	_____	_____	___/___/_____
___/___/_____	_____	_____	_____	___/___/_____
___/___/_____	_____	_____	_____	___/___/_____
___/___/_____	_____	_____	_____	___/___/_____

VET VISIT

DATE: ___/___/_____   AGE: _____

   WEIGHT: _____   HEIGHT: _____

VISIT PURPOSE:

_____

_____

_____

TESTS DONE:

_____

_____

_____

DIAGNOSIS:

_____

_____

_____

MEDICATION:

_____

_____

_____

VET VISIT

DATE: ___/___/_____   AGE: _____

WEIGHT: _____   HEIGHT: _____

VISIT PURPOSE:

_____
_____
_____

TESTS DONE:

_____
_____
_____

DIAGNOSIS:

_____
_____
_____

MEDICATION:

_____
_____
_____

VET VISIT

DATE: ___/___/_____   AGE: _____

WEIGHT: _____   HEIGHT: _____

VISIT PURPOSE:

_____

_____

_____

TESTS DONE:

_____

_____

_____

DIAGNOSIS:

_____

_____

_____

MEDICATION:

_____

_____

_____

VET VISIT

DATE: ___/___/_____   AGE: _____

WEIGHT: _____   HEIGHT: _____

VISIT PURPOSE:

_____

_____

_____

TESTS DONE:

_____

_____

_____

DIAGNOSIS:

_____

_____

_____

MEDICATION:

_____

_____

_____

VET VISIT

DATE: ___/___/_____   AGE: _____

WEIGHT: _____   HEIGHT: _____

VISIT PURPOSE:

_____

_____

_____

TESTS DONE:

_____

_____

_____

DIAGNOSIS:

_____

_____

_____

MEDICATION:

_____

_____

_____

VET VISIT

DATE: ___/___/_____   AGE: _____

WEIGHT: _____   HEIGHT: _____

VISIT PURPOSE:

_____

_____

_____

TESTS DONE:

_____

_____

_____

DIAGNOSIS:

_____

_____

_____

MEDICATION:

_____

_____

_____

VET VISIT

DATE: ___/___/_____   AGE: _____

   WEIGHT: _____   HEIGHT: _____

VISIT PURPOSE:

_____

_____

_____

TESTS DONE:

_____

_____

_____

DIAGNOSIS:

_____

_____

_____

MEDICATION:

_____

_____

_____

VET VISIT

DATE: ___/___/_____   AGE: _____

WEIGHT: _____   HEIGHT: _____

VISIT PURPOSE:

_____
_____
_____

TESTS DONE:

_____
_____
_____

DIAGNOSIS:

_____
_____
_____

MEDICATION:

_____
_____
_____

VET VISIT

DATE: ___ / ___ / _____   AGE: _____

WEIGHT: _____   HEIGHT: _____

VISIT PURPOSE:

_____

_____

_____

TESTS DONE:

_____

_____

_____

DIAGNOSIS:

_____

_____

_____

MEDICATION:

_____

_____

_____

VET VISIT

DATE: ___/___/_____   AGE: _____

WEIGHT: _____   HEIGHT: _____

VISIT PURPOSE:
_____
_____
_____

TESTS DONE:
_____
_____
_____

DIAGNOSIS:
_____
_____
_____

MEDICATION:
_____
_____
_____

VET VISIT

DATE: ___ / ___ / _____   AGE: _____

WEIGHT: _____   HEIGHT: _____

VISIT PURPOSE:

_____

_____

_____

TESTS DONE:

_____

_____

_____

DIAGNOSIS:

_____

_____

_____

MEDICATION:

_____

_____

_____

VET VISIT

DATE: ___/___/_____   AGE: _____

WEIGHT:_____   HEIGHT: _____

VISIT PURPOSE:

_____

_____

_____

TESTS DONE:

_____

_____

_____

DIAGNOSIS:

_____

_____

_____

MEDICATION:

_____

_____

_____

VET VISIT

DATE: ___ / ___ / _____   AGE: _____

WEIGHT: _____   HEIGHT: _____

VISIT PURPOSE:

_____
_____
_____

TESTS DONE:

_____
_____
_____

DIAGNOSIS:

_____
_____
_____

MEDICATION:

_____
_____
_____

VET VISIT

DATE: ___/___/_____   AGE: _____

WEIGHT: _____   HEIGHT: _____

VISIT PURPOSE:

_____

_____

_____

TESTS DONE:

_____

_____

_____

DIAGNOSIS:

_____

_____

_____

MEDICATION:

_____

_____

_____

VET VISIT

DATE: ___ / ___ / _____   AGE: _____

WEIGHT: _____   HEIGHT: _____

VISIT PURPOSE:

_____

_____

_____

TESTS DONE:

_____

_____

_____

DIAGNOSIS:

_____

_____

_____

MEDICATION:

_____

_____

_____

VET VISIT

DATE: ___/___/_____   AGE: _____

WEIGHT: _____   HEIGHT: _____

VISIT PURPOSE:

_____
_____
_____

TESTS DONE:

_____
_____
_____

DIAGNOSIS:

_____
_____
_____

MEDICATION:

_____
_____
_____

VET VISIT

DATE: ___/___/_____   AGE: _____

WEIGHT: _____   HEIGHT: _____

VISIT PURPOSE:
_____
_____
_____

TESTS DONE:
_____
_____

DIAGNOSIS:
_____
_____
_____

MEDICATION:
_____
_____
_____

VET VISIT

DATE: ___/___/_____   AGE: _____

    WEIGHT: _____   HEIGHT: _____

VISIT PURPOSE:

_____

_____

_____

TESTS DONE:

_____

_____

_____

DIAGNOSIS:

_____

_____

_____

MEDICATION:

_____

_____

_____

VET VISIT

DATE: ___/___/_____   AGE: _____

WEIGHT: _____   HEIGHT: _____

VISIT PURPOSE:

_____

_____

_____

TESTS DONE:

_____

_____

_____

DIAGNOSIS:

_____

_____

_____

MEDICATION:

_____

_____

_____

VET VISIT

DATE: ___/___/_____   AGE: _____

WEIGHT: _____   HEIGHT: _____

VISIT PURPOSE:

_____

_____

_____

TESTS DONE:

_____

_____

_____

DIAGNOSIS:

_____

_____

_____

MEDICATION:

_____

_____

_____

VET VISIT

DATE: ___/___/_____   AGE: _____

        WEIGHT: _____   HEIGHT: _____

VISIT PURPOSE:

_____

_____

_____

TESTS DONE:

_____

_____

_____

DIAGNOSIS:

_____

_____

_____

MEDICATION:

_____

_____

_____

VET VISIT

DATE: ___/___/_____   AGE: _____

WEIGHT: _____   HEIGHT: _____

VISIT PURPOSE:

_____
_____
_____

TESTS DONE:

_____
_____
_____

DIAGNOSIS:

_____
_____
_____

MEDICATION:

_____
_____
_____

VET VISIT

DATE: ___/___/_____   AGE: _____

     WEIGHT: _____   HEIGHT: _____

VISIT PURPOSE:

_____

_____

_____

TESTS DONE:

_____

_____

_____

DIAGNOSIS:

_____

_____

_____

MEDICATION:

_____

_____

_____

VET VISIT

DATE: ___/___/_____   AGE: _____

WEIGHT: _____   HEIGHT: _____

VISIT PURPOSE:
_____
_____
_____

TESTS DONE:
_____
_____
_____

DIAGNOSIS:
_____
_____
_____

MEDICATION:
_____
_____
_____

VET VISIT

DATE: ___/___/_____   AGE: _____

WEIGHT: _____   HEIGHT: _____

VISIT PURPOSE:

_____

_____

_____

TESTS DONE:

_____

_____

_____

DIAGNOSIS:

_____

_____

_____

MEDICATION:

_____

_____

_____

VET VISIT

DATE: ___/___/_____   AGE: _____

WEIGHT: _____   HEIGHT: _____

VISIT PURPOSE:

_____

_____

_____

TESTS DONE:

_____

_____

_____

DIAGNOSIS:

_____

_____

_____

MEDICATION:

_____

_____

_____

VET VISIT

DATE: ___/___/_____   AGE: _____

WEIGHT: _____ HEIGHT: _____

VISIT PURPOSE:

_____
_____
_____

TESTS DONE:

_____
_____
_____

DIAGNOSIS:

_____
_____
_____

MEDICATION:

_____
_____
_____

VET VISIT

DATE: ___/___/_____   AGE: _____

WEIGHT: _____   HEIGHT: _____

VISIT PURPOSE:
_____
_____
_____

TESTS DONE:
_____
_____
_____

DIAGNOSIS:
_____
_____
_____

MEDICATION:
_____
_____
_____

VET VISIT

DATE: ___/___/_____   AGE: _____

WEIGHT: _____   HEIGHT: _____

VISIT PURPOSE:

_____

_____

_____

TESTS DONE:

_____

_____

_____

DIAGNOSIS:

_____

_____

_____

MEDICATION:

_____

_____

_____

VET VISIT

DATE: ___/___/_____   AGE: _____

WEIGHT: _____   HEIGHT: _____

VISIT PURPOSE:

_____
_____
_____

TESTS DONE:

_____
_____
_____

DIAGNOSIS:

_____
_____
_____

MEDICATION:

_____
_____
_____

VET VISIT

DATE: ___ / ___ / _____   AGE: _____

WEIGHT: _____   HEIGHT: _____

VISIT PURPOSE:

_____

_____

_____

TESTS DONE:

_____

_____

_____

DIAGNOSIS:

_____

_____

_____

MEDICATION:

_____

_____

_____

VET VISIT

DATE: ___/___/_____   AGE: _____

WEIGHT: _____   HEIGHT: _____

VISIT PURPOSE:

_____
_____
_____

TESTS DONE:

_____
_____
_____

DIAGNOSIS:

_____
_____
_____

MEDICATION:

_____
_____
_____

VET VISIT

DATE: ___/___/_____   AGE: _____

WEIGHT: _____   HEIGHT: _____

VISIT PURPOSE:

_____

_____

_____

TESTS DONE:

_____

_____

_____

DIAGNOSIS:

_____

_____

_____

MEDICATION:

_____

_____

_____

VET VISIT

DATE: ___/___/_____   AGE: _____

WEIGHT: _____   HEIGHT: _____

VISIT PURPOSE:

_____
_____
_____

TESTS DONE:

_____
_____
_____

DIAGNOSIS:

_____
_____
_____

MEDICATION:

_____
_____
_____

VET VISIT

DATE: ___/___/_____   AGE: _____

WEIGHT: _____   HEIGHT: _____

VISIT PURPOSE:

_____

_____

_____

TESTS DONE:

_____

_____

_____

DIAGNOSIS:

_____

_____

_____

MEDICATION:

_____

_____

_____

VET VISIT

DATE: ___/___/_____   AGE: _____

WEIGHT: _____   HEIGHT: _____

VISIT PURPOSE:

_____

_____

_____

TESTS DONE:

_____

_____

_____

DIAGNOSIS:

_____

_____

_____

MEDICATION:

_____

_____

_____

VET VISIT

DATE: ___/___/_____   AGE: _____

WEIGHT:_____   HEIGHT: _____

VISIT PURPOSE:

_____

_____

_____

TESTS DONE:

_____

_____

_____

DIAGNOSIS:

_____

_____

_____

MEDICATION:

_____

_____

_____

VET VISIT

DATE: ___/___/_____   AGE: _____

WEIGHT: _____   HEIGHT: _____

VISIT PURPOSE:

_____

_____

_____

TESTS DONE:

_____

_____

_____

DIAGNOSIS:

_____

_____

_____

MEDICATION:

_____

_____

_____

VET VISIT

DATE: ___/___/_____   AGE: _____

WEIGHT: _____   HEIGHT: _____

VISIT PURPOSE:

_____

_____

_____

TESTS DONE:

_____

_____

_____

DIAGNOSIS:

_____

_____

_____

MEDICATION:

_____

_____

_____

VET VISIT

DATE: ___/___/_____   AGE: _____

WEIGHT: _____   HEIGHT: _____

VISIT PURPOSE:

_____
_____
_____

TESTS DONE:

_____
_____
_____

DIAGNOSIS:

_____
_____
_____

MEDICATION:

_____
_____
_____

VET VISIT

DATE: ___/___/_____   AGE: _____

    WEIGHT: _____   HEIGHT: _____

VISIT PURPOSE:

_____

_____

_____

TESTS DONE:

_____

_____

_____

DIAGNOSIS:

_____

_____

_____

MEDICATION:

_____

_____

_____

VET VISIT

DATE: ___ / ___ / _____   AGE: _____

WEIGHT: _____   HEIGHT: _____

VISIT PURPOSE:

_____

_____

_____

TESTS DONE:

_____

_____

_____

DIAGNOSIS:

_____

_____

_____

MEDICATION:

_____

_____

_____

VET VISIT

DATE: ___/___/_____   AGE: _____

    WEIGHT: _____   HEIGHT: _____

VISIT PURPOSE:

_____

_____

_____

TESTS DONE:

_____

_____

_____

DIAGNOSIS:

_____

_____

_____

MEDICATION:

_____

_____

_____

VET VISIT

DATE: ___ / ___ / _____   AGE: _____

WEIGHT: _____   HEIGHT: _____

VISIT PURPOSE:

_____
_____
_____

TESTS DONE:

_____
_____
_____

DIAGNOSIS:

_____
_____
_____

MEDICATION:

_____
_____
_____

VET VISIT

DATE: ___/___/_____   AGE: _____

WEIGHT: _____   HEIGHT: _____

VISIT PURPOSE:

_____
_____
_____

TESTS DONE:

_____
_____
_____

DIAGNOSIS:

_____
_____
_____

MEDICATION:

_____
_____
_____

VET VISIT

DATE: ___/___/_____   AGE: _____

WEIGHT: _____   HEIGHT: _____

VISIT PURPOSE:

_____

_____

_____

TESTS DONE:

_____

_____

_____

DIAGNOSIS:

_____

_____

_____

MEDICATION:

_____

_____

_____

VET VISIT

DATE: ___/___/_____   AGE: _____

WEIGHT: _____   HEIGHT: _____

VISIT PURPOSE:

_____
_____
_____

TESTS DONE:

_____
_____
_____

DIAGNOSIS:

_____
_____
_____

MEDICATION:

_____
_____
_____

VET VISIT

DATE: ___/___/_____   AGE: _____

WEIGHT: _____   HEIGHT: _____

VISIT PURPOSE:

_____

_____

_____

TESTS DONE:

_____

_____

_____

DIAGNOSIS:

_____

_____

_____

MEDICATION:

_____

_____

_____

VET VISIT

DATE: ___/___/_____   AGE: _____

WEIGHT: _____   HEIGHT: _____

VISIT PURPOSE:

_____
_____
_____

TESTS DONE:

_____
_____
_____

DIAGNOSIS:

_____
_____
_____

MEDICATION:

_____
_____
_____

VET VISIT

DATE: ___/___/_____   AGE: _____

WEIGHT: _____   HEIGHT: _____

VISIT PURPOSE:

_____

_____

_____

TESTS DONE:

_____

_____

_____

DIAGNOSIS:

_____

_____

_____

MEDICATION:

_____

_____

_____

VET VISIT

DATE: ___/___/_____   AGE: _____

WEIGHT: _____   HEIGHT: _____

VISIT PURPOSE:

_____

_____

_____

TESTS DONE:

_____

_____

_____

DIAGNOSIS:

_____

_____

_____

MEDICATION:

_____

_____

_____

VET VISIT

DATE: ___/___/_____   AGE: _____

WEIGHT: _____   HEIGHT: _____

VISIT PURPOSE:

_____
_____
_____

TESTS DONE:

_____
_____
_____

DIAGNOSIS:

_____
_____
_____

MEDICATION:

_____
_____
_____

VET VISIT

DATE: ___ / ___ / _____   AGE: _____

    WEIGHT: _____   HEIGHT: _____

VISIT PURPOSE:

_____

_____

_____

TESTS DONE:

_____

_____

_____

DIAGNOSIS:

_____

_____

_____

MEDICATION:

_____

_____

_____

VET VISIT

DATE: ___/___/_____   AGE: _____

WEIGHT:_____   HEIGHT: _____

VISIT PURPOSE:

_____
_____
_____

TESTS DONE:

_____
_____
_____

DIAGNOSIS:

_____
_____
_____

MEDICATION:

_____
_____
_____

VET VISIT

DATE: ___ / ___ / _____   AGE: _____

    WEIGHT: _____   HEIGHT: _____

VISIT PURPOSE:

_____

_____

_____

TESTS DONE:

_____

_____

_____

DIAGNOSIS:

_____

_____

_____

MEDICATION:

_____

_____

_____

VET VISIT

DATE: ___/___/_____   AGE: _____

WEIGHT: _____   HEIGHT: _____

VISIT PURPOSE:

_____
_____
_____

TESTS DONE:

_____
_____
_____

DIAGNOSIS:

_____
_____
_____

MEDICATION:

_____
_____
_____

VET VISIT

DATE: ___ / ___ / _____   AGE: _____

WEIGHT: _____   HEIGHT: _____

VISIT PURPOSE:

_____
_____
_____

TESTS DONE:

_____
_____
_____

DIAGNOSIS:

_____
_____
_____

MEDICATION:

_____
_____
_____

VET VISIT

DATE: ___/___/_____   AGE: _____

WEIGHT:_____   HEIGHT:_____

VISIT PURPOSE:

_____

_____

_____

TESTS DONE:

_____

_____

_____

DIAGNOSIS:

_____

_____

_____

MEDICATION:

_____

_____

_____

VET VISIT

DATE: ___/___/_____   AGE: _____

    WEIGHT:_____   HEIGHT: _____

VISIT PURPOSE:

_____

_____

_____

TESTS DONE:

_____

_____

_____

DIAGNOSIS:

_____

_____

_____

MEDICATION:

_____

_____

_____

VET VISIT

DATE: ___/___/_____   AGE: _____

WEIGHT:_____   HEIGHT: _____

VISIT PURPOSE:

_____
_____
_____

TESTS DONE:

_____
_____
_____

DIAGNOSIS:

_____
_____
_____

MEDICATION:

_____
_____
_____

VET VISIT

DATE: ___/___/_____   AGE: _____

WEIGHT: _____   HEIGHT: _____

VISIT PURPOSE:

_____

_____

_____

TESTS DONE:

_____

_____

_____

DIAGNOSIS:

_____

_____

_____

MEDICATION:

_____

_____

_____

VET VISIT

DATE: ___/___/_____   AGE: _____

WEIGHT: _____   HEIGHT: _____

VISIT PURPOSE:

_____

_____

_____

TESTS DONE:

_____

_____

_____

DIAGNOSIS:

_____

_____

_____

MEDICATION:

_____

_____

_____

VET VISIT

DATE: ___ / ___ / _____   AGE: _____

WEIGHT: _____   HEIGHT: _____

VISIT PURPOSE:

_____

_____

_____

TESTS DONE:

_____

_____

_____

DIAGNOSIS:

_____

_____

_____

MEDICATION:

_____

_____

_____

VET VISIT

DATE: ___/___/_____   AGE: _____

WEIGHT: _____   HEIGHT: _____

VISIT PURPOSE:

_____
_____
_____

TESTS DONE:

_____
_____
_____

DIAGNOSIS:

_____
_____
_____

MEDICATION:

_____
_____
_____

VET VISIT

DATE: ___/___/_____   AGE: _____

   WEIGHT:_____   HEIGHT: _____

VISIT PURPOSE:

_____

_____

_____

TESTS DONE:

_____

_____

_____

DIAGNOSIS:

_____

_____

_____

MEDICATION:

_____

_____

_____

VET VISIT

DATE: ___/___/_____   AGE: _____

WEIGHT: _____   HEIGHT: _____

VISIT PURPOSE:

_____

_____

_____

TESTS DONE:

_____

_____

_____

DIAGNOSIS:

_____

_____

_____

MEDICATION:

_____

_____

_____

VET VISIT

DATE: ___/___/_____   AGE: _____

    WEIGHT: _____   HEIGHT: _____

VISIT PURPOSE:

_____

_____

_____

TESTS DONE:

_____

_____

_____

DIAGNOSIS:

_____

_____

_____

MEDICATION:

_____

_____

_____

VET VISIT

DATE: ___ / ___ / _____   AGE: _____

WEIGHT: _____   HEIGHT: _____

VISIT PURPOSE:

_____

_____

_____

TESTS DONE:

_____

_____

_____

DIAGNOSIS:

_____

_____

_____

MEDICATION:

_____

_____

_____

VET VISIT

DATE: ___ / ___ / _____   AGE: _____

WEIGHT: _____   HEIGHT: _____

VISIT PURPOSE:

_____

_____

_____

TESTS DONE:

_____

_____

_____

DIAGNOSIS:

_____

_____

_____

MEDICATION:

_____

_____

_____

VET VISIT

DATE: ___/___/_____   AGE: _____

WEIGHT: _____   HEIGHT: _____

VISIT PURPOSE:

_____

_____

_____

TESTS DONE:

_____

_____

_____

DIAGNOSIS:

_____

_____

_____

MEDICATION:

_____

_____

_____

VET VISIT

DATE: ___/___/_____   AGE: _____

WEIGHT: _____   HEIGHT: _____

VISIT PURPOSE:

_____

_____

_____

TESTS DONE:

_____

_____

_____

DIAGNOSIS:

_____

_____

_____

MEDICATION:

_____

_____

_____

VET VISIT

DATE: ___/___/_____   AGE: _____

WEIGHT: _____   HEIGHT: _____

VISIT PURPOSE:

_____

_____

_____

TESTS DONE:

_____

_____

_____

DIAGNOSIS:

_____

_____

_____

MEDICATION:

_____

_____

_____

VET VISIT

DATE: ___ / ___ / _____   AGE: _____

    WEIGHT: _____   HEIGHT: _____

VISIT PURPOSE:

_____

_____

_____

TESTS DONE:

_____

_____

_____

DIAGNOSIS:

_____

_____

_____

MEDICATION:

_____

_____

_____

VET VISIT

DATE: ___/___/_____   AGE: _____

WEIGHT: _____   HEIGHT: _____

VISIT PURPOSE:

_____
_____
_____

TESTS DONE:

_____
_____
_____

DIAGNOSIS:

_____
_____
_____

MEDICATION:

_____
_____
_____

VET VISIT

DATE: ___/___/_____   AGE: _____

WEIGHT: _____   HEIGHT: _____

VISIT PURPOSE:

_____

_____

_____

TESTS DONE:

_____

_____

_____

DIAGNOSIS:

_____

_____

_____

MEDICATION:

_____

_____

_____

VET VISIT

DATE: ___/___/_____   AGE: _____

WEIGHT: _____   HEIGHT: _____

VISIT PURPOSE:

_____

_____

_____

TESTS DONE:

_____

_____

_____

DIAGNOSIS:

_____

_____

_____

MEDICATION:

_____

_____

_____

VET VISIT

DATE: ___/___/_____   AGE: _____

    WEIGHT: _____   HEIGHT: _____

VISIT PURPOSE:

_____

_____

_____

TESTS DONE:

_____

_____

_____

DIAGNOSIS:

_____

_____

_____

MEDICATION:

_____

_____

_____

VET VISIT

DATE: ___/___/_____   AGE: _____

WEIGHT:_____   HEIGHT: _____

VISIT PURPOSE:

_____
_____
_____

TESTS DONE:

_____
_____
_____

DIAGNOSIS:

_____
_____
_____

MEDICATION:

_____
_____
_____

VET VISIT

DATE: ___/___/_____   AGE: _____

    WEIGHT:_____   HEIGHT: _____

VISIT PURPOSE:

_____

_____

_____

TESTS DONE:

_____

_____

_____

DIAGNOSIS:

_____

_____

_____

MEDICATION:

_____

_____

_____

VET VISIT

DATE: ___/___/_____   AGE: _____

WEIGHT: _____   HEIGHT: _____

VISIT PURPOSE:

_____

_____

_____

TESTS DONE:

_____

_____

_____

DIAGNOSIS:

_____

_____

_____

MEDICATION:

_____

_____

_____

NOTES:

NOTES:

NOTES:

NOTES:

NOTES:

NOTES:

NOTES:

NOTES:

_____
_____
_____
_____
_____
_____
_____
_____
_____
_____
_____
_____
_____
_____
_____
_____
_____
_____
_____
_____
_____
_____
_____
_____

NOTES:

NOTES:

NOTES:

Made in the USA
Las Vegas, NV
02 March 2024